A Full Bag

Written by Caroline Green
Illustrated by Ángeles Peinador

Collins

a big hat

a top

a big hat

a top

her bag
• • •

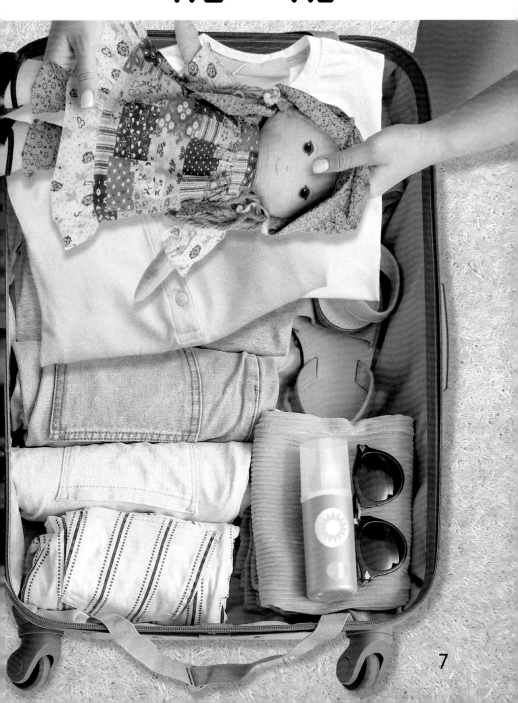

her bag

pack the doll

and a red cap

toss in socks

and a red cap

🐾 Review: After reading 🐾

Use your assessment from hearing the children read to choose any GPCs, words or tricky words that need additional practice.

Read 1: Decoding

- Turn to page 7 and ask the children to read the text. Ask if they can spot the digraph that makes the /c/ sound (*ck*).

- Turn to page 10 and, covering the final "s", invite the children to read the word "sock". Then uncover the "s" and ask them to read it again, ensuring they sound out the final "s" correctly to read **socks**.

Read 2: Vocabulary

- Look back through the book and discuss the pictures. Encourage children to talk about details that stand out for them. Use a dialogic talk model to expand on their ideas and recast them in full sentences as naturally as possible.

- Work together to expand vocabulary by naming objects in the pictures that children do not know.

- Ask the children to read page 7. Ask them to point to and read the word that explains what they are packing. (***doll***)

- On page 10, point to **toss** for the children to read. Ask: What does this mean? (*throw, chuck*)

Read 3: Comprehension

- Turn to pages 14 and 15 and ask the children to talk to you about what has been packed in the suitcase. Ask them if they can see any items that they recall from the book. Ask the children: What type of holiday do you think she's going on? (*hot/beach holiday*) What makes you think that? (*towel, suncream, etc*)

- Invite children to talk about any holidays they've been on. Ask: Where did you go? What did you take with you? What were you most pleased that you took?